A Young Upstart

Contour Drawings and Poetry: 1977-1982

Ron Cook

A Young Upstart

Contour Drawings and Poetry: 1977-1982

Ron Cook

Ron Cook Studios Publishing

A Young Upstart

Second Edition | October 2023

Ron Cook Studios Publishing
www.roncook-author.com

These poems are works of fiction. Any references to historical events, real people, or real locales are used factually. Other names, characters, places and incidents are the product of the author's imagination, and any resemblance to actual events or locales or persons, living or dead, is entirely coincidental.

Trade Paperback ISBN 979-8-9892128-0-4
eBook ISBN 979-8-9892128-1-1

Printed in the United States of America

To all those who journeyed down a dark, depressing path then found a map to take them back to the light. For me, that map was the book, Gestalt Therapy Verbatim, by Fritz Perls (1893-1970).

Gestalt therapy is a client-centered approach to psychotherapy that helps clients focus on the present and understand what is really happening in their lives right now, rather than what they may perceive to be happening based on past experience. Instead of simply talking about past situations, clients are encouraged to experience them, perhaps through re-enactment. (I re-enacted through drawing and writing.) Through the gestalt process, clients learn to become more aware of how their own negative thought patterns and behaviors are blocking true self-awareness and making them unhappy.

Acknowledgments

The drawings, poetry, and stream-of-consciousness writings in this book began in 1977 and helped pull me out of a period of self-doubt and self-pity. What inspired me to start self-therapy were the books and teachings of Fritz Perls, especially <u>Gestalt Therapy Verbatim</u> and <u>In and Out of the Garbage Pail</u>.

Contour drawing was taught to me during my first year as an art major at Gavilan College in 1964. The technique stuck with me.

I made most of the drawings and writings in this book at the Upstart Crow Bookstore and Coffeehouse in the Campbell Pruneyard from 1977 to 1980. The rest I created at Pergolesi's Coffeehouse after moving to Santa Cruz in 1980.

I find it quite impossible to thank everyone who encouraged me to write and who shared their expertise and suggestions over the years, especially my wife, Stella, a long-time book fan, who has also been my long-time fan. (I'm her long-time fan.) Her encouragement and help have kept me typing away.

1.
Fall into a sleepy daydream state of mind
Couldn't help myself
    …reality was hard to find
Star man smiled and waved his hand
    …played by some band
Thoughts escaping
All relating
Some are fading memories of pleasure
        …rarely experienced.

2.
You may be searching forever (to find what's not there),
You are ready to go (but you never know why),
Fortune could smile on you any old day,
(But you're afraid she will laugh when you die.)

3.
It's been so long since we were parted
Now I feel your heart beating
Seems by now we should have started
Time to end our daydreaming.
At last I touch, and you are feeling
It took so long to reach that goal
You play a tune, my mind is reeling
It struck down to my very soul.

4.
What is past has transpired.
Expired.
Retired into maturity.
Sought after for so long,
unconsciously yearning for all.
Wanting everything,
Getting some.
Escaping into oblivion,
Spreading it too thin.
Ice broke through,
Many times pursuing
Extravagant dreams,
Never ending,
Never again.

Reality
(a familiar word by now)
Speaks for us all.
Few hear the cries of anguish
From
The disheartened,
Thoroughly upset
Crowds milling around in the misery
They condemned themselves to.
Were not we
Who see
Once blind
As they
(my horn is blowing)
Are not the blind leading the crippled?
Are not the crippled leading the totally invalid?

Advanced notice.
Change affliction
For infection
For defection.
Rising ever slightly,
Slow processes.
Some will joyfully emerge.
Some not.
Some unhappily start again.

Only one
Can be one
Can help one set one straight.
Assimilate.
Consummate.

Fritz,
Impasse,
Overpass

"Would you mind turning the light back on?"

5.
Perhaps.
Find the solution to a problem
Never lasting
Always there were times at future gatherings
Unfolding
Untold
Unnerving
Unending
Unreasonable
Undermined thoughts by DeSade
Drifting by
Lastly
Into porous retainers
Left up to the Greeks
No way to size up
To work up
To make up
To pack it up
To leave fucking establishment
Behavioral patterns
Lighting from above
Maximum endurance

Minimal actions
Speaking words
Relaying nothing but visual images
Stoned images
Mindless images in stone and paper
Laced up to the knees
Past the zenith
Apex
Crown
Point of no returning
To reality
Escaping fantasy
Viewers undo said approach
To runway
Far away
Underlying
Over lying
Every aspect of nature's laws
Intended to coerce any piper
Pied
Keeping in form
Formless Formica
Formulated
Fornicated
Faster
Fucker
Feelings enough
Never enough
Relating
Non-relating
Under captions
Thought balloons
Popping off
Hm-m-m-m
I see
Said the blind man groping for an answer
Inside he knows.
And yet…

6.
Another barroom heartbreak
Left the floor in the heat of the game
The name of the game is not the same
As before.
I can hear the creative juices flowing.
Fresh squeezed.
Every time I call you up to ask you out, you're on vacation.

7.
Peaceable kingdoms in my soul
It is not my body that is beckoning
Reaching for quantities unknown
The growing child reaching out
    …for the growing imagination.
Hard to laugh in a peaceable kingdom
    …boredom develops
    …boredom envelopes
Reaching out of the peaceable kingdom
Reaching out of boredom
Hands get caught and enfolded amongst all the reachers
    …everyone is bored
    …everyone is reaching.

An impasse in their lives and the shared life
Some would like to go through
    …adventurous
    …dangerous
Some want to bypass
    …not adventurous
    …secure
The boredom has been cancelled
For the moment.

The peaceable kingdom in my soul
Is not so peaceable after all.
Anxiety treads there
Doubt, insecurity stomp through in view of your mind's eye
Exclamatory questions
     …wh?
     …wh?
     …wh?
And why?
Doubt of ability
Insecure is present thoughts
And anxious over when they shall happen again

The condemned man ate a hearty last meal.

8.
Packed into a velvet box
Watching My life go by in seconds

Can this really be happening to Me?
Or am I dreaming
(doesn't ease Me)
daydreams never come true
can this really be happening to Me?
Can this really be happening?
Can this really be?

Matching actions
    …by actions
only so far until one breaks
breaking
help
(but no one can help Me except for myself)
    "Let me lend you a hand then."
thank you
    "You're welcome."

9.
Lest I forget My ungodly ways
And head up the path for so many days
The nights aren't the same indoors or out
So I have a mind and the feeling to shout
  …right out loud into the air
  …but people will stop, and many will stare
Embarrassed easy
Time to leave
Drunken mind
I start to weave

Doors open and shut.

10.
Life as it is ain't much to behold
    …yet,
but no life at all is a poor plaything
When all who exist look to you
    …when you're not there
Only a void and unanswered questions
    …standing in a non-shadow
Existing here only for oneself
Any pleasure someone gets is secondary

We need the attention of others for our existence
We are hermits although we intended to leave/live on our own
We need people around to give our lives strength
Attention
    …from others
Love
    …from others
The physical need
The need for companionship
The need for love.

11.
Realization. Ha!

Cynicism's showing, isn't it?

Descriptive passages read with a friend,
Cynical lines wondered about.
Winter bareness
Warm sun
No rain
A brown January
Avoidance.
Look inside too much,
Blow up

Warped.

12.
Best friends often part
    …unconsciously,
Seeing
    …but not seeing
Feeling
    …but not feeling
Being together
    …but not together
    …anymore.

13.
Party at the local dead-end,
Too late for a date.
How do you rate?

Hours turn into days to eternity
Flying higher than ozone breeze
And life's short term lease
Dancing the night away
But then
The party's only started
At the local dead-end

It can happen again
Never comes to a head
Enough has been said…

A likeness becomes the undeterminable man
Making hard scenes harder
Dumb ones smarter
Come on.
Come.
They're dancing the night away
But then
The party's only starting
At the local dead-end.

14.
Dysphoria

I could cry
   …if only I could think of something to cry about.
Life by itself is not worth the bother,
Nor are the problems I pile on myself.
So why must I grieve over the best there is?

Time
And Time again,
Unsure thoughts emerge from within,
Where they should stay until you are sure…
   …of yourself

15.
Passing the time reviewing each other
    …and our works
Warm January thought of rain and release.

I admit you write better than I.
Moving images.

No wind today.
Dry pods hanging from the mimosa tree.
Like a thousand tiny bats.
Paul Rogers trying to be poetic
    …and sing at the same time.

16.
Leaving this life
And
Entering the next.
Behaving like a grownup
For a change of pace.
Sitting up nights and days,
Become less and less,
Until
The time arrives,
Again,
For a person/child
Desperately in need of recognition,
And,
The fact of the matter,
Recognition is there
But,
Rejected.

Stream #1
I hope you're satisfied with the position of grace I've been forced
into seeing things I never imagined something like this could have
happened to a person like myself getting involved involuntarily
momentarily divided by the scope of the crux of the matter of fact
I saw one the other day laying its feet in the snow birds and water
fowl speech giving and taking advantage of the wonder women
working wherever womankind wanders quietly and listens to the
windward leeward monkey ward off evil spirits speak beak least of
all chatter aimlessly breaking ties with ethereal beings reeking
ectoplasm and death heads knowing and you must answer me now
go.

17.
How can you tell the world how you feel
When you can't tell yourself?
I can tell,
With the help of others

18.
Describing thoughts is too easy.
Is that why I do it?
The scenario takes effort,
And
Effort is time consuming.
Ventures lose interest.
The change is so slowly he turned,
Step by step,
Inch by inch,
I struggle to maintain a readable structure,
But,
What of images cast aside,
Asunder.
A sure thing
No image is there.
Words appear in the mind's eye
Groping for felling
And,
With the feeling there,
I should also have a visual picture.
But,
How do you visualize words?
Except as words.

19.
Should I give up today and try again on the 'morrow?
Or
Should I give up and try on the 'morrow again?
And
Again, I write words as they dribble out of my pen,
Which is the finest 49 cent nylon tip pen available,
That
Lets the paper squeak under the pressure
I so laboriously exert upon its poor framework,
    Groaning from over-repeated clichés.
Dangling metaphors.
Run-on sentences.
Dingleberries.

And,
All around poor grammar.
And,
Spelling wasn't much of a strong point
In my younger days I could spell quite well,
Which was understandable because of the high intellect
Told I had
I took for granted.
Until,
School got boring,
As it does for most geniuses (me?)
Could never stand idiot teachers.
Drove me crazy with misinformation.
Dull subjects.
Times are tough,
Eh,
Bud?

20.
I feel
?
I experience feeling
?
I
Am full
Of
Sensual
Awareness
?
Sensitivity
Emanates
From
My aura
?
Practically
All
My
Pores
Ooze
Sensitive
Feelings
?

I
Have
More
Feeling
In
My
Little
Finger…
?
I'm
More
Sensitive
With
Sensual
Feelings
Than
You
?
I
Am
Aware
Of
More
Sensual
Awareness
Emanating
Sensitivity
From
My
Limbs
?
I
Experience
Feeling
?
?
I
Feel!

21.
Salvaging
The remaining efforts brought you into the air
Space
Birth
Death
Infinity
Leaving
Believing
Grieving
Yet screaming out for others to hear me
See me
Feel me
Copyright infringement
Left for dead
Someone said
So…
So, what said someone
Dead for left field funnies
Fanny Brice
Eating rice

Playing dice
Breaking ice
Deviant slice of life's blood
Flowing into the veins of babes
In arms
The alarm has rung
The song was sung
Ring out the old ways
Left by the way side
Lined up against the odds
Makers bet
Caretakers get
Shareholders wet their beds
In dreams of sexual ecstasy
Groans of relief
Moans from the brief encounter groups
In therapy
Groping for answers
   …help
Help yourself
Trial and error
Needing a spare
Conscience is talking back to me
And
Myself as the example
Look back no more
Look ahead
Into the past
Glories
Speak for themselves
After a fashion
Manage to change the look of a country
A world turns
A few into plastic
Elastic
Fantastic
Fantasized
Lovers greeting each other
Orgasm

Leave out the important images
Left by man-child
Left on the steps
Greeted by the household as their own image
God's image
God's eye
Mind's eye
The same image in both sides
Now
Have we at last sighted
Legless
Armless beings
Minus torso and head
Lines forming
Tears falling
Outside the rain falls
Wood smoke
Car smells
Cat spray
Light the fire
Drifting off
Dozing off
Jacking off to the sound of one hand
Clapping
Slapping the thighs
High again
Keep me warm
Getting warmer
Warmest
EXPLODE!
    …sigh
?
Write, write, write
Scribble
Scrawl
Scratch…
    …uh
Write, write
Scribble

Scratch, scratch…
    …sigh
Mother of pearl wherever you've gone
Mother of pearl I pray to thee
Save me from the righteous wrong
Save me from the likes of me
And
Myself
And
Thyself
HOLD ON IT'S COMING!
    …again?
Slappa, slappa, slappa
False alarm
Drifting
Again
And
Again
    …and again.

22.
Pleasant.
Blossoms
Odors of orange
Odors of almond
Odors of acacia
Premature odors for this time of year.
Warm days
Cool nights
The sap is beginning to flow again
    …and again

Pleasant.

23.
Lively banter requesting thrust
Into maelstrom envy becoming thus
Last and least it requires age
Not the start, but the turn of the page
Leaving units and angry fire
Wanton lust requires ire
Working gingerly passive rhymes
Accepting anything, time and time.
Again, the quiet seeks you out
Searches past a silent scout
Cash and carry 'til death parts you
Necessary gender 'twas thus "I do"

Party's started, don't be late
Check the action, speculate
Anxiously waiting for answers inside
Purposely dodging the ones you can't hide
Neat and aw-reet found the right one at last
Pounding the pudding a blast from the past
Visual stimuli reeking of sweat
Take everything in, it's all you can get
Chance upon rivalry never again
Put sword in hand, either prick or the pen.

24.
Receiving pleasure past the pain
Enables loves release to gain
Popular votes cast inside me
Strike against monopoly.
Resurgent sources gather under
Prying eyes leave time to wonder
Paying homage to the image I cast
More precious than all the kinds that last.
Friendships burdens seem smaller now
I've reached inside to find somehow
The love I lost, or thought was gone
Returned once more.

25.
Apart
Yet
   …near in my heart
The longing
   …so alone
Yet filled
   …with the joy only love could bring.

26.
Locked inside a thin-skinned shell,
The secret of life
The end of hell.
    A made to order primal scream!

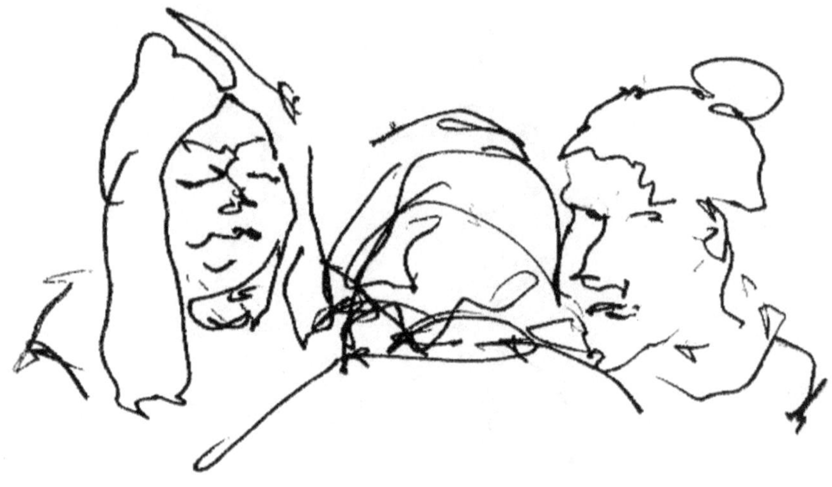

27.
Again, in the midst of the crowd
The soft noise of talking
Friends and lovers
Hopeful and hopeless
Studious, plaintive
Yet all share in the common room
Shouldn't they know all?
Each other speaking freely
Overheard tight mouthed courses
Free the voice
Free the people
Free your minds to each other.

28.
Myself
With my life on the walls
Surrounding this room
The identities of old
That were hiding in the gloom
     Stored inside unknown to myself
     Playing music with words of despair
     Brought on by not knowing
     Yet knowing too much
     Yet not trying to care.
With an urge to advance
On a life taking shape
A new one, a better one
The one destined by fate
     Stored inside unknown to myself
     Playing music with words of despair
     Brought on by not knowing
     Yet knowing too much
     Yet not trying to care.

Reaching out now
Improving with years
The life taking shape
Well past the fears
       Stored inside unknown to myself
       Playing music with words of despair
       Brought on by not knowing
       Yet knowing too much
       Yet not trying to care.

29.

The Experiment
More than before with the time that has past
The friends have become the strangers at last
Working against the rules of the game
Working, but results end up the same.
>As before
>Try as you can
>It remains the same
>As before
>You're telling yourself
>You're sorry you came.
In view along with the rest of the crowd
Into the maze, don't be so proud
Avoiding life as you find it outside
And closing your mind by trying to hide
You'll never escape. There's too many here
And you say that things can't be as clear.

As before
Try as you can
It remains the same
As before
You're telling yourself
You're sorry you came.
Along for the wild and unforgettable ride
Along to weep or cheer those who tried.
Along to be born, but not to die
Along to speak truth, but trying to lie.
As before
Try as you can
It remains the same
As before
You're telling yourself
You're sorry you came.

30.
The evening's gone by and we wait for the dawning
My lips they keep moving, but you're have been yawning
Lately I've barely kept my head above all the water
And lately you have focused on mother and daughter.
Role playing
We're both saying
Sharp tongues
But we're both still young.
Role playing
Yet laying
Together
Always wondering out loud
Learning from each other in the time we spend
Together like trees in the wind, we bend
Still, friends and lovers are strangers in the end.
We've won and lost, we're children still growing
We grow wild in the streets with the oats we've been sowing

My lips are still moving and yours are still yawning
The evening's gone by but we'll wait for the dawning.
Try to keep from role playing
We're both saying
Thoughts out loud
Alone in a crowd
Keep from role playing
We're both laying
Together
We'll always wonder
Keep learning from each other in the time we spend
Together, like the trees in the wind, we bend
Still, friends and lovers are strangers in the end.

31.
Lasting inquiries injured party
Unnerved into policy holder related
Species hot chocolate pretending
Dance procedure ever lasting
Happy endings creating perpetuated
Ideas of closeness deftness hazards
Ahead the last the best keep the
Faith under the circumstances dating
False prophecies under the weather
Deter the fact of the matters get worse
Before better feelings endeavors
Create escalate excelsior.

32.
I've passed up my friends
They are falling behind.

With a book in my hands
Reflecting on the insecurity long passed
Down the end of another road
No questions asked
No questions asked

No questions asked in the thought balloons
The answers have come and gone
Reasons for living and reasons for giving
Another reason for song.

33.
Let the daydreamer sleep into the dawn
Close the eyes seeking solution
Actively searching with limited bounds
Each thought just adds more confusion.

Soul searching seeker, you're killing the ego
That fed upon life as you found it.

Day after day brings the nearness of death
A release that's not rushing to find you
A direction of sorts should be forming inside
By leaving the bonds you were tied to.

Many have tried
Unclaimed and untied
Chanced to wander outside
Hope in changing the tide
To themselves they have lied
An existence to ride
Seeking to hide
Gave up and died

Soul searching seeker, you're killing the ego
That fed upon life as you enjoyed it.

All the clues to the life that you dream of at night
Lay bunched up and are screaming to leave you.

Lost in a spellbound uncertainty
Presence endearing reality
Pressing on press on dear one
Parting old ways creating the
New life endangered enraptured
Frightened of the initial onslaught
Leaving left frightened of the
Secondary
The third
The final
Finally comfortable in the dreams of seduction and truthful
tales of love one another to be as one another at another time

Pasteboard figures cut from the ether.

34.
Smiling happy concerns
No crying for untied ends
Deeply in love with life currently
Impotent but not indignant
Lonely but not lonely with myself
At the moment anyway.

35.
Dreaming sadly dreaming away
Concern for life drifting into other
Thoughts of love tender closeness
Warmth greets lovers.

36.
Milo wept as they carried the pall
He wept as he dreamt of the future
Desires, burning, enflamed
Crying to hide his own danger
Crying to hide
Sadness inside
As he was feigning emotion
Doubt on his face
Caused the mind to erase
And left him to proceed without caution.

37.
Anxiety ridden jaws tight with hope
Searching the pavement and trying to cope
Wanting to love but remaining well hid
Dreams of the feel and the touch of her hand
Are all I have left.
They were there from the start.

38.
Ashes to ashes
and dusk to dawn,
The feeling's inside,
but the outside?
It's gone.

Stream #2
The easiest way to my own enlightenment is through my own enlightenment I once believed in myself only as a person and not a personality only an object filling space falling in space no life of my own no mind of my own no, I had a mind but I had not the inclination to use it every change was brought about by shock things change around me that I have to think about I was forced to think the collapse in self-pity, self-abuse and a growing hatred for the games of the living.

Stream #3
Suicide many times entered my unattended psychological ramblings much pain and pressure where did this pain and pressure go?
Their disappearance usually comes from the passing of time but the continuance of the events that caused more than time to extinguish the hell brought on mostly by myself.
Awakening.
An explosion that cleansed the interior of my skull from the infection of 29 years of misinformation street learning ego and an apathy of sorts then real life was forced into me I think of myself as a personality now there was a goal in my life that was missing before not a sexual goal but realistic material goal aesthetic on its learning and finish my contribution of beauty to this dying planet many problems still remain but the mind works constantly to solve these never again will my brain cells atrophy into mush.

    They will work for their living.

    I will work toward my living.

    I will work toward my life.

39.
I can see how the day ends
The light disappearing
The sun goes down again and again.

My life goes like light
Every day darkness entering
The sun goes down again and again.
The sun goes down again.

Daytime goes fast
Not enough for the asking
The sun goes down again and again.

Darkness condemns one to searching,
Reflecting.
The sun goes down again and again.
The sun goes down again.

Peace in the light keeps my mind energetic,
Why must the sun go down again.
Night brings on thoughts of
Lost love so pathetic,
Why must the sun go down again
Why must it go down again.

Dreaming of love leaves me hurt and depressed,
I'll never want to die and let the darkness overwhelm.
But the sun goes down again one last time.

40.
Exasperating sequence of events
Consumed by Arabs living in tents
Meeting the keepers around and around
Dreaming of sleep. Abound.

41.
At last the dream came as I soaked the sheets twice over the cool
dampness of sweat and the damp coolness of life's fluid.
The dream came as I softly, so sweetly, she was there, reaching out,
her touch felt real.
Wake up embracing air.
Relaxing feverishly curled in a heap.
Her presence was felt long before sleep,
when sleep came
she stood beside me with a cheetah close by she had turned free.

42.
He circled the block a second time just so he could get another look
at the young lady in the bikini standing in her front yard.
A common thing for him to do considering his in-bred horniness.
Horny because he doesn't fuck enough (by his standards).
Horny because his wife is puritanical while he reads all the latest
on sex in the skin mags.
Horny because he imagines the masculine image to be in bed with
a seductress every evening for life,
and he's not keeping up his part of the image.
Horny because every woman is trying to be seduced,
he thinks,
but he can't get into the action because he's married too hard.
His imagination travels to all locales of the world in exotic sexual
flings only pictured occasionally in his magazines.

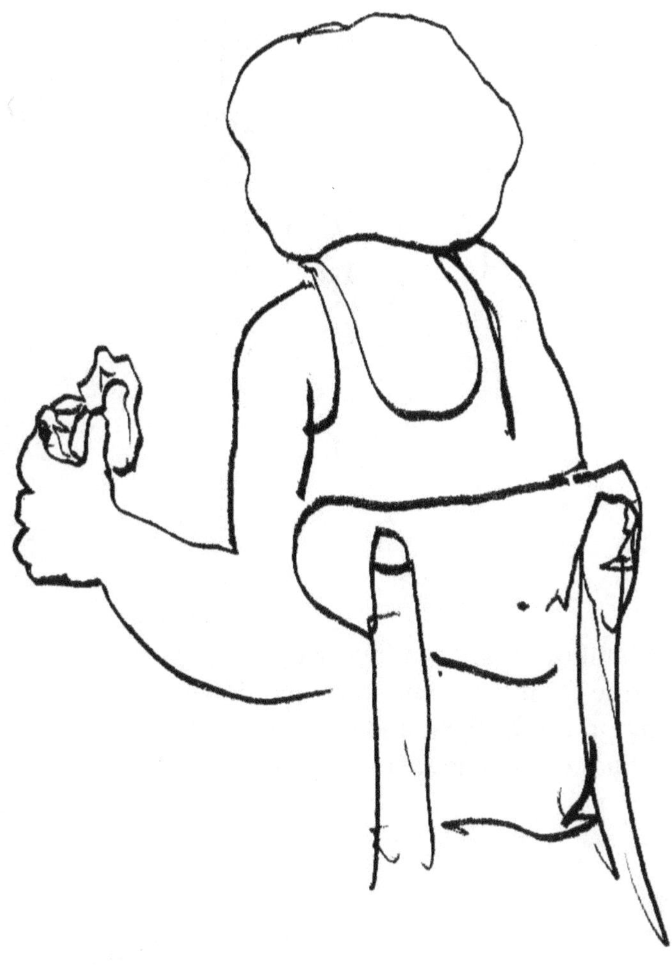

43.
Permanence remains without a doubt
Love ventures through the curtain to give the audience a taste of
envy.
Undisturbed in the thought yet disturbed
Wanting more of the same others wanting give and take.
Personal remembrances purified
Yet joyous well being displayed from the course of events.
What more, to write on except for that's experienced.

44.
Partly fault of ours, never every one,
Rings true for most, sometimes overdone,
Singing praise for liars, and every liars' son,
Partly fault of ours never every one.

45.
Open shop,
Out at second.
Ego drop,
Out at third,
Momentum stop.
Out at home,
Call the cops. He's killed himself.

46.
I left home at an early age,
Searching for life and a hairy sage,
Kept up my travels 'till death called my name,
Tore me from life and put an end to my game.

Stream #4

Look here and there why can't we be the best of friends or the kindest enemies travel together beholding hands down thumbs down get down old sage in the brush kind man travel hurry pretty thing curly hair very cute short hair long dress summer gown please don't frown look here and there why can't we be the best of friends or the kindest kindred kinship leaving normal passages of times own extravagant yearnings yearly yeast infection in the dark foreboding enemy agent left under over sideways down pretty thing girl person looking fresh wanting outdoors closed up problems no hopefully saying I to you pretty thing sitting there alone with your book I shall not bother I'm afraid to bother you pretty thing look here and there why can't we be the best of friends or the kindest figure of speech walk through disappear pretty thing sitting there coffee plain no sugar no cream cigarette doesn't look natural for you pretty thing Shirley MacLaine eyes short hair tall thin pretty thing sitting there brown hair dark eyes upturned nose pretty thing sitting there and here why can't we be the best of friends for the kindest lack of communication but sight is pleasing wanting pretty thing sitting there relaxed feet up in the chair framed in wicker body pleasing smile pretty thing sitting there your book is interesting engrossed so pretty thing sitting there why can't we be friends I'm in love with a vision no more to see after these brief moments pretty thing your life is unknown to me my life to you so to remain.

47.
Revolting to say the least.
I never saw a life I could enjoy more than mine
Only improvements to this model could please me more.
Improving constantly.
Someday the time will come when learning ends.
Death.
Not that pleasant and not that good is the prospect of death.
But what of death? Is it as bad as has been said?
Remember back to the time before your birth. What was it like?
You don't remember?
Than it couldn't have been all that bad.

48.
The Conscience Goes Round and Round
Dangers in excess of the norm
Keeps a man down unable to perform
Desire reaps caution, a lack of well being
Lust causes actions with or without seeing
Fire in eyes perhaps making friction
Writers indulge putting fact on the fiction
No no Nanette cries of anguish abound
Yes yes the conscience goes round and round
Guilty inside for small escapades
Hide all the feelings a play of charades
Alone by yourself wishing for death
Premature action! Life's all you have left.

49.
Left for dead
someone said
keep your head
get out the lead.

Stream #5
Travel past untold monuments left to the real help most tread there when what who left grade the class joker wild mild change the glass blowing gypsy joker clap crap ahead of a chance clap trap reach breach the rest tired tell aggressive pretext barrister chance mucho macho perhaps leaving soon left.

Stream #6
Drumming it into my brain damage uncontrolled into extreme hardships coming in someday the procession proceeds to creep under ivy trained particles of call girls reeking gently over tricks of the trade winding your way slowly toward the mountain of devils and rapists fat fuckers getting a rock off the coastline at twilights last gleaming roses smelling of musk and fruit scents into dollars and pennies worth the sacrifice if only mother was cool in the beginning and father had the guts to stand on his own while I went on and on by myself in my room with the radio folk songs Ross McGowan KSJO had its day sometimes past with never a dull day afternoon spent working in the orchards the horses have a pleasant odor emanating.

50.
Songs have been related to society's past
Equated with life and misery birth and death
Forever the tune rambles on and on and on with each breath
Never recorded but sounded since birth
What was it worth?
The tune always changes
The song remains the same
Before and after release the poet
Integrity perhaps will render the novice to sing out his verse
It couldn't be worse than singing one note as loud as he can
Again and again.
Enough has been said.
The poet is dead.
That one anyway.
This one is very much alive.
Almost time to drive away again to the other life.
Stories emerge. Only problem is to translate thoughts to structure to images on paper.
Time will be the teacher.

Stream #7

Momentarily gain haze sex dreams lovely girls leaving breath short trying dying inside yearn free I'm free but restraint keeps me from diving into the maelstrom of human relations forever churning into a frothy sight unseen seemly mature lovely sex dreams never wet dreams soaking eternal scum cum come magma cum laude voice scream inside to touch love under the influence of personal hygienic confluence conditioned partitioned lengthened strengthened hand insertion peg board love affair sight love driving force stripped years.

51.
Mucho Ado Over Nothing
Partly at fault probably completely
Was it necessary from the start
Should it have been so discreetly
Lovely creatures demanding views
Personal choice a mulligan stew
Saint Pat or Vitas dancing away
Crosses to bare nearly everyday
Perhaps said again and again it was said
Left all alone, still better than dead.

52.
Another story is that person sitting not really alone together senior citizen was it worth it?
Perhaps, then maybe not.
Only he knows the truth.

53.
What's His Life?
The drawing looks like Lincoln.
But he looks more like a hip IBM employee.

54.
I Used to Pass for Dead
I used to pass for dead in my head
I used to stay alive, shuck and jive
It took a nervous breakdown to make the best for myself and for the
concerned individual.
Left again by others.
Sisters, brothers.
It was not a bother, at all.
Lovely day everyone has been saying too much too soon a
modulation of the seasons
Intelligent beings we, but selfish to the core
It's a whore.
Baltimore.
Nevermore.
Distant shore.

That's not too intelligent leaving the structure and wandering off the path of thought.
Bought.
Caught.
A lot of people come and go.
I for one have wanted to know
The trial is real.
The jury unjust.
Terminate the spirit
Or the body will bust.
Never fear,
The way is clearly envisioned amongst the revelers and downers and uppers and clowners and fixers and wreckers and chessman and checkers.
Last but not least there remains double deckers
Out of the gloom.
Bride of the groom.
Entangled. Entrapped.
And stuck on the lap of human kindness sticking erect pointed eject anointed indulge demise and diverge.
I left home at the early age of twenty and eight
Respect for my elders declining of late.
I know it would happen, yet I did not prepare for the trauma.
I was yet to envision as reality coming and going down slipping
Thighs cries of anguish and holes in the walls.
I couldn't stall anymore
She went her way then came back
To the original insert who became the deserter
Insecurity reigned supreme as the survey from one to another to another then back continued to entrap and contaminate.

55.
There is a wealth of information from every person everywhere.
A story from each, maybe more than one.
It will never be done.
An impossible task that would be,
To chronicle the life of every person you meet.
Shit! Not at all what I wanted.
Intended for life not as a biographer,
But as a musician, poet, woodworker, master of all.
An artist, a man of the world.
If there is time, a millionaire, if the money would be there.

56.
The time has come replied the devil.
To leap into the flames of unpassionate desire.
Uncontrollable lapse of memory
Leaving the chance for controllable desire.
Meanings slip
Perhaps they trip up sedate warring individuals
Last but least calling rise to Hermaphrodite both and one
Undone undone
Undone once again crying for life to give birth
Realization comes too late.
What was the worth of lying to achieve goals unholy.
Holy, holy, an atheist's curse
To die just to find that life's a lot worse.
Falling in dreams
Forever it seems

Until hitting the floor of reality and the blood stops flowing
Through veins long turned cold
A nightmare in life, daydreaming in death
Born again to rise and fall under the burdens you developed the
last time around.
Do you realize what you have done?
Do you realize you have fallen under your own gun?
One plus one plus one is one
Nothing left to do but run into
Another corner of your box
Like a castrato wondering at your worth
Sun on your shoulder rejected since birth
Inborn
Inform
Rebirth
Fall again into the life and death struggle
The long dead mind regenerates to die again.
Shortly to live
Finally, to die the last.

Parting of Souls
Parting of souls
Many in one
Premature goals
Almost undone.

Stream #8

Laughter abounds in a world of celestial thought reasoning actors speak violently consoling every person seeking a reeling body in the night of passion playing vermin rocking rolling past unquiet souls parched or frozen depths of Mordor ring seekers fictional journeys keep the blood flowing fluid surging throngs in view of changing emotions constantly endangering the life inside outside rangers CB call bears woods beer bar guzzle guzzle drifting returning patrons consenting adults rafters full of scantily clad undone vehicles of social digesting 10cc flower of womanhood corporate image kept up understood masculine image kept up not understood too well sought after noting remains but the remainder of life's never always ending perfunctory imperfect subjects to need not need reject inspect lie cheat indulge devour shit ugh— constipated balls of marbles of little round brown grass seasons end summers ahead life anew spring time emotions young man's fanciful endeavors cloaked in my sternum travelers surely they jest you know they don't ever consider only pleasures in themselves does size counts large larger largest of all thrust bearing straight into the chasm train tunnel smoke stack apparition succubus incubus non-real wetdreams abound around astound wake up covered with cream cheese soaked bagels and waffles syrup ooze squeeze bottle trickle trickle hot dogs and burning logs every morning forgetting then remembering hot to trot jog jog jog look as that's where it's at memorable for the moment by moment unwarranted sightings erect stature erecting statue after the fall call only where the need arises arise Sir Trots-a-lot.

57.
Song/Poem

"In the Shadows of a New Year"

In the shadows from some other time,
Some other love, some other thoughts in mind.
Gasping for the last grasp on life,
On the follies, on the thought of being a part of it all.

It's in the shadows,
It's in the shadows with time.

News and views of the other kind,
Other dramas, other bittersweet curves and lines.
Another rebellious youth disengaged himself from life,
From living, from being a part of it all.

It's in the shadows,
It's in the shadows with time.

Lusting hearts selling souls by the thousands,
By the way, buy some bread on the way home tonight.
Women and men torn apart, brought together,
Brought under, brought about by being a part of it all.

It's in the shadows,
It's in the shadows with time.

58.
Song/Poem

"Xmas in March"

Minimum balance and maximum waste,
The flavor is gone, it was bad for the taste,
The caption had read, "Don't eat library paste,
It might give you a cramp or the worms".

Left in a hole without water or bread,
Keeping awake with a bump on your head,
Lacking in style, but enough has been said,
Vote that guy back another term.

Please, please look away,
I'm neither straight, bi-sex, or gay,
Don't knock me down, the ground is too hard,
You want to play? Come into my yard.

Blonde upon blond passes by only once,
Stare back and smile, it's okay, stupid dunce,
To think about loving and not about cunts,
Don't you know that I'm one of a kind?

Assortments of all that may wander this way,
Just one or two to be queen for a day,
What would I do if it's not for a lay?
Who knows, I'm not in that bind.

Please, please look away,
I'm neither straight, bi-sex, or gay,
Don't knock me down, the ground is too hard,
You want to play? Come into my yard.

Wonderful news comes too far between,
The lines on my face, you know what I mean,
About peaches and cream and a reason to scream,

What is it I need? What's the score?
Later in life the same dollar appears,
As a muse in green gowns lifted up to his rear,
My, how I wander, the end must be near,
Time to close down, lock the door.

Please, please look away,
I'm neither straight, bi-sex, or gay,
Don't knock me down, the ground is too hard,
You want to play? Come into my yard.
Please, please look away,
The curse is in living, day by day,
Falling love, the eyes they do strain,
Ah, fuck, it's beginning to rain.

59.
Incorrigible, incurable lover of the fair sex, sexist attitudes aside, looking artistically, aesthetically, pleasing to the eyes. Occasional love/lust emotional disorders fantasizing innumerable escapades all for the pleasure of one who wants to please all.

> Alone in a crowd,
> Reaching out for recruits,
> Silently speaking aloud
> Hoping to suit
> Every one of you
> In my dreams I do scream,
> With every one of you
> Going insane with the pleasures every man craves
> With every one of you.
> Wanting every one of you.
> The pain's so intense it's love for sure this time
> With every one of you.

Every day on the streets
Eyeing all who appeal,
Hoping for smiles to greet
And a chance to seal
With every one of you.

All the years of my age,
Produced so few,
All the world's a stage,
With you, and you, and you.

60.

Song/Poem

"The Man is a Child"

The never-ending search for the perfect life,
Prompts man to hide his fears,
Hope upon hope keeps him crying inside,
The feeling will last many years.

And many times more he will doubt his choice,
And many times more he will ask himself why,
Many times will beget many more,
It could go on 'till he dies.

The man is a child,
Spontaneous and wild,
Aggressive then mild,
Always needing someone.

The man's still a boy,
Engrossed with the toys,
He finds hard to enjoy,
Without the help of someone.

When will he see all that is obvious?
When will he grow on his own?
When will he open his mind like his eyes?
When will he see that he's grown?

But many times more he will doubt his choice,
And many times more he will ask himself why,
Many times will beget many more,
It could go on 'till he dies.

The man is a child,
Spontaneous and wild,
Aggressive then mild,
Always needing someone.

The man's still a boy,
Engrossed with the toys,
He finds hard to enjoy,
Without the help of someone.
Always needing someone.
Always needing someone.

61.
Song /Poem

"Mister Nothing Man"

Mister nothing man,
Have you made up your mind another time,
To become a something man?
Have you cleaned up your act,
To become a positive man?

You've been nothing for years,
Now you can't hide the tears,
Brought out by the fears,
Of the things you steered clear of.

Mister nothing man,
In your fashionable clothes
No one likes but those close,
'Cause they're lying, man.
You've been taught the wrong way every day,
All your teachers come back to haunt you, man

You've been nothing for years,
Now you can't hide the tears,
Brought out by the fears,
Of things you steered clear of.

Mister nothing man,
Be a something man,
At least learn one thing, man,
And be a something man,
Mister nothing man.

Mister nothing man
Accomplishing very little,
It's a puzzle you don't wake
The little giant inside you, man.

You've been nothing for years,
Now you can't hide the tears,
Brought out by the fears,
Of things you steered clear of.

Mister nothing man,
Be a something man,
Learn one thing, man,
Be a something man.

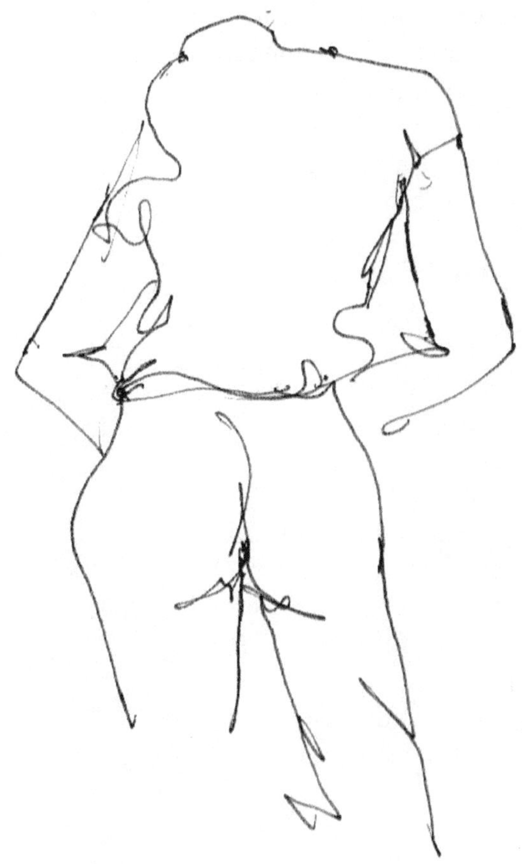

62.
Song/Poem
"A Reflection on You"

As you stand before your bathroom mirror,
Running fingers through your cardboard hair,
Brush and floss your pearly ivory cluster,
Watch the faces changing there.

It's only in your mind dear,
It's all in your mind,
It's only in your mind dear,
It happens all the time.

A vision peering through the steam and moisture,
The fog distorts the face you see in there,
Licking lips that hide in condensation,
Put a kiss upon the mirror.

It's only in your mind dear,
It's all in your mind,
It's only in your mind dear,
It happens all the time.

Close your eyes,
Your vision's still inside there,
Close your eyes,
The fog has disappeared,
Close your eyes,
And slowly leave the bathroom,
And the face behind the mirror.

It's only in your mind dear,
It's all in your mind,
It's only in your mind dear,
It happens all the time.

63.
I am dreaming again
And scheming again
Planning my life away
Wishing for some other day
    To come along.
    A day that can't go wrong.
    The perfect time
    To pass this life of mine away.
    Someday.

I am in a trance again
I'll have to make a stance again.
All this will have to pass
Get up off my ass.
    Plan my life
    Sort out all the strife
    In my head
    If I can ever get out of bed again.
    Today

Thinking about the perfect day
And the dues I've had to pay
When I've had nothing to say,
Looking ahead for that perfect day.

I am drifting again
Spirit's lifting again
Could be happier in the dreams
Much more pleasant so it seems
    But then again
    It's neither there or when
    Clear my mind
    Take the time to unwind
    Someday.

Try to unwind again
Someday
That could be the perfect day
Someday.

64.
To the end of eternity
And the dreams of posterity
Knock twice verily
Think hard hazily.

Back off from vulgarity
Praise posthumously
But not entirely
With thoughts unknowingly.

Praise be
To me
We see ourselves as heroes and villains.

With ideas soaked with pride,
Thinking we're along for the ride,
And the crowd's yelling "Slide!"
Bury your head and hide.

The idea's inside could have died,
And the people you love could have lied,
Don't give up before you've tried,
You can take it all in stride.

Praise be
To me
We see ourselves as heroes and villains.

Stream #9

What's the use of waiting in the auto when what's the use is the
final plea the final grace in this place for ever under asunder the
wonderful gratuitous affair of state of the art clear cut and under
fire by the state of siege ensuing the desperate channels of
boredom conducting himself with a 12-piece highly illuminated
(Blake) orchestra and turnstile percussion reverberating through
the auditorium making the sound of music annoying as grocery
store Muzak filtering through the rows of vegetables and cocoa
pebbles with applause and thunderation the exclamation of the
poor souls were deafening the right ones and the wrong ones
barely able to keep up life's pace without crumbling the goodness
left through their boot heels to be wandering meandering with
doubt before a search could ensue to you into prime time
reasoning not concerning anyone in particular as mother's pride
soaks like milk toast under a downpour of tears that are mostly
reptilian in the dominion that you assume yet cannot examine for
the lights not right to write yet why not you say as the son's set
southerly to your moonscape silhouette as no one in particular in
your enemy and everyone is suspect.

65.
Whisper to her again,
Show her quietly what you want and feel from her.
Hide with her again,
The coast is clear to go your way and meet with her.
Greet her.
Speak with her to say what you've wanted to tell someone all along.
Love her.
Lay with her.
The dream recurs so often, there is not a chance it could be wrong.
The two of you.
One to love and one to live out the fantasy.
The two for you.
Unsure of staying for want of living the fantasy.
Dream of her.
Sleep and move from fantasy to the other as often as time will let you.
Go to her.

You want, so why not take that which has been handed to you.
They both want you.
You want them too.
One knows all.
One hides in her invisible shell and waits for you to call.
Inside yourself.
The nervous existence fights for release.
You're beside yourself.
Your energy flow shows a need for release.
So, love her.
And lay with her.
Your dream recurs so often there is not a chance it could be wrong.
Love her.
Lay with her.
Stop the dream and make the fantasy come true,
Because they both belong to you.
One to love.
One to live out the fantasy.

66.
I saw the need and the seed grew.
I tried to work and the jerk in me knew,
Of by-laws and changes
And dog-eared pages,
Leather-bound volumes of forgotten prose,
And poetry for the masses,
Some of it passes
Off as good at times.

Once upon a time and a dime short later,
Marriage on the rocks and the cock's much softer,
From crowing too early
And getting too surly,
A tasty little sucker
In preparation for late night feasting
Occasional teasing,
It's good at times.

It was fast and the last I knew
The trials went late and as fate drew
The messages
The passages,
Again, dog-eared pages
Paperback used volumes
Everyone's favorite prose
Quick sold to the masses
Without hassles,
It's as good as it could be.
See?

67.
The lady I've got to believe in
Leaves her mark everywhere she goes
We hardly have time for each other,
She's the one I don't even know.

Sweet music was written just for you,
And the poems sing your praise every night.
I would be very lonely without you,
And to be so alone isn't right.

With a time that you use for reflection,
And a time that your wishing for love,
If I just had one chance to be with you,
It's like reaching for stars above.

You're so busy,
Will you every see me,
Will love ever see me.
I'm always dreaming,
Will you ever see me again.

Stream #10

I had hopes of meeting someone new for a change of pace and in keeping with the laws of nature's own indiscriminate use of chemicals to make us all pure there was also hope of promising myself to stop this and go back to that only not that far back to shut off all that was learned.

Stream #11

At a time when all good things end, all that lies before me is good. All intentions are honorable, and all endeavors are for the good and pleasure of others.

68.
Sexist Psychobabble…
Asses were made for bearing…
Women were made for bearing…
Barring any more conflicts unending the real and the unreal who are susceptible to only and all illnesses of the mind and/or body.
Eject, erect, ejaculate into vials for future populations super science superman endeavor.
Leave well enough alone they say to procreate as the creator meant.
Look under that cabbage leaf.

Stream #12

Enter with grace the solitary ace in the game by the name of something or else dying in front of the crowd in spite of the pall and the shroud covering stage left to the right just in sight of eager believers insipid transvestite orgies inure the wrath of graft succeeding preceding unending pastimes not withstanding yet idle chatter doth beget idle chatter suspect and inspect morally endangered greeting card sellers at your door perhaps a whore under the brown suit straining to emerge the butterfly in the soldier cocoon needing and needed and perhaps learning a bit on someone's flowing aura glowing tingle into quiver out of a new image draining the old. Perhaps... the new reigning over the old. Perhaps....

69.

Thought

Would you care to join me in a quiet afternoon of four, five, or six play? I'm tired of one-play.

Thought 2

The abundance of compromise has catapulted the relationship into a lifetime of happy non-marriage. Always seeking acceptance and never accepting what was closest.

Thought 3

To music my mind stays always, as with acquaintances with new and beautiful ladies.

Thought 4

To have as I want would be to live boredom, and to live boredom is death in the mind.

70.
Song/Poem
"Something is Waiting"

Something is waiting out there,
Something is always waiting,
To rip your expectations.
Something is waiting out there,
Something is always waiting,
At the edge of desperation.

It will strike out hard and grab you by your heart,
And hold it like some easy gentle prey,
Its voice will echo through some empty hallways,
What it will tell you there no one will ever say.

But who told you this life would be easy,
Has he money so he never has to care?
That man will never pull you up from down under,
Rise up yourself, if you dare, if you dare, if you dare.

Something is waiting out there,
Something is always waiting,
The chance is in the taking.
Something is waiting out there,
Something is always waiting,
No choice, and there's no faking.

There's just nowhere to run for any cover,
That's not the only thing that you could do,
Who knows what evil lurks in the hearts of men here?
Scatter yourself and something will find you.

I never told you this life would be easy,
I've no money and I really do care,
I'll help you anyway I can and pull you up from down
under,
I'll help you rise, if you dare, if you dare, if you dare.

71.
Song/Poem
"Love Made in Heaven"

The two of you were Siamese from the start,
You are the twins of love that are joined at the heart,
No one will find one without one by your side,
I thought it weird but now I'm letting it slide.

Because it's love made in heaven,
Love made in heaven,
Love made in heaven. Ah…

I doubt if I could be as close as you are,
No one has love like yours that's traveled this far,
My nerves go up in flames when loving too long,
I look at you two and I wonder what's wrong.

I don't have love made in heaven,
Love made in heaven,
Love made in heaven. Ah…

You've proven love can last without any fear,
You never look annoyed by being too near,
I wish my mind would take a lesson from you,
But if I'm stuck with one, I've nothing to do.

You need love made in heaven,
Love made in heaven,
Love made in heaven. Ah…

I try to see myself inside of your shoes,
The little man in me says what can you lose,
But I get a funny feeling somewhere down here,
It's crowds of two or more that bring on my fear.

I don't have love made in heaven,
Love made in heaven,
Love made in heaven. Ah…

Stream #13

Lonely days lonely nights where would I be without my (women) lady friends and lady strangers lady fingers I love to hold in keeping with traditions settings to warm the stares that start out cold.

72.
Song/Poem

"I Noticed You Yawning"

Your moods aren't new to me,
I've written songs about your kind many times before,
But I fall so ungracefully,
For every interesting girl that walks in the door.

You know I lust someway after every girl,
Is that normal for a guy of my years?
I want to know all about their lives,
But when I talk about mine, it bores them to tears.

I noticed you yawning,
You're tired, I can tell you're tired of me already.

You all are so beautiful,
I want all of you I can get,
I smile, but you look the other way,
This is going to be the death of me yet.

If only you were different somehow,
If we could find a common ground,
But I distinctly get the feeling,
You don't want me around.

I noticed you yawning,
You're tired, I can tell you're tired of me already.

73.
Song/Poem
"Voyage of the Greasy Slinger"

Standing in a doorway,
Laying in a pew,
'tis a greasy slinger there,
Not appearing new.
'tis a greasy slinger there,
On a slate so clean,
On a slimy billiard cue,
Eating gormy bean.

"What say?" quoth I,
To he, be she or it.
"Must you lay in your nappy,
Or nap be on you sit?
I've seen you mop a gurney,
And cart a crackle fop,
But never in a doorway,
Or pew be on you spot."

"Fuzz ye!" to I say he,
Voice and tongue both bitie,
Kite and loper aimed at thus,
Many of them mighty,
"Pour forth unto poppy lot,
And cook greers until goldy,
Sacks and flowers kindled keed,
Nacks and goodgies mouldy."

So I left the temple pert,
And being in the cruelly,
Port a miley kilo too,
And sought a booby truly,
On to Dooty Ebiner,
And past the gate of prime…

Falling down a homigal,
Then I woke in time.

Stream #14

Acres of silk without all the charming hundreds of children breaking the calm down to the dreadlock braided with mud a lark splashes into water emerging converging with either/or nothing/something coming out of oneness within/without perpetrated to bring still others under the wing everything flows/grows into the mass confusion coordinated to be yet seeing the life flowing on ever on into pools of shallow thought and ponds of indecisive images cast to boggle the mind and let thee be under/asunder thunder clap (clap, clap, clap) sounding with two people in mind never mind the one whose least concerns you have not lived until you have died of old age from the cage that was built and fortified with the tears of no one in particular so perhaps a tear should fall but not on so happy an occasion alley cats will cry and scratch until, until… perhaps all is vanity as they say. Perhaps all is a dream as they say. Perhaps no more should be said… as they say. No… as you say.

Stream #15

I could be sitting here for days on end and still be better for the worse things that could happen would be the termination of the sense I rely on the most.

Not to see the passing of beautiful people (and to laugh inwardly at the not so beautiful) would be a crime against my nature. My very soul would be torn from me.

Yet—do I not suffer from anxiety when I view a beautiful girl?

Do I not wish she would smile, talk, invite me along with her for some beautiful memory making journey into a sexual/fantasy environment realized only in the most beautiful of erotic fiction?

If I were blind, I would never have to go through these fantastic meanderings. I would dream but not see the possibilities.

I would have to be content with myself and those I know already.

I dare not go on.

Stream #16

What an idea it was to become the idiot avenger has been until the force of gravity brought reality unto or into or out the weary soul searcher into a vile contrasting conjecture with the feeling of life before birth control set the undoer undone while many more creatures of the life style fat source create undo while make believe and set the next down into optional according to whom where how and why fore not through creative force do not elude my efforts to stylize lines into some tangible evidence as one or more search the identity inside before the outside can say one sentence like what else is new so are you yet if this is living I must be alive or the figment of some artist's vivid imagination.

74.
Years ago, she led me far along with my knowing.
She kept me where my mind could go on growing.
Without my knowledge or my help
And my dreams of instant riches
She stayed to lend a hand
And mend the broken pieces
Of my shattered hopes.

75.
Old men who stare
Old ladies who glare
At youthful exuberance
At beauty, where they had no chance
Look at the world here
With personalities near
Comparisons all
Rivals in life,
The old song and dance.

76.
Left on the edge of the final term
Searching forever under the sheets
Over the streets
Apart from the nearest neighboring fact or fiction
Requires an age of unending learning never ceases to
Amaze your friends influencing people into believing
Only the last was the least anticlimactic of all the
Climaxes fall short impotent fools
Searching forever under the sheets
Over the streetwalker's distasteful ooze down
Come down
Fall down
Fall short of expectations
Wham, bam, thank you ma'am
The influence of never coming together again scares the hello
Out of fools rushing in will lapse into uncontrollable fits of
Disgust and love
Why win
No winners ever forever
Under the sheets
Over the streets
Manly ego deflate, inflate, deflate, berate
Belittle the bastard searcher lover under cover
Thankful dealings outward feelings

Inward, outward
Monkey Wards laughter reigns, feigns
Aiming for an early withdrawal of troops
An epidemic known but avoided
Too touchy, risky
Keep out of sight seers and underdogs relating to the end of life
As the black hole sexiness void
Balls off
Count off
Jack off all trades
Exchanging eye for eye
Aye, 'tis the assumption of few that many remain the norm
Out of view
Can it be the hard nose, hard assed, wise ass keeps up his guard
Only to expose his balls to the constant bludgeoning castration
Complex
Unique
Eunuch fear of homosexual yearnings
Fuck up
Caught up in someone else's lifestyle creating your own blown
Out by an inferior detail
Suck
Fuck
Duck the blows
Torn between immortality and death as a famous person or persons
Impersonating the end of life as the beginning of a new learning
Forces yourself to be the example
Up against the wailing wall
Over extended
Over pretended
Over dependent
(Out of the mouths of babes in the woods)
Fires burning
Cleansing one
Establishing an environment for another.

77.
Now that the time has kept going
Contrary to what has been said
And more time can be expected
Now that we can see where it led

So far time has deluded me
So far time has gone through my fingers
So far time has flown
Time and time again we say.
Yet it never lingers

Never have I seen it
And I've never felt it
Yes, it's always there
It lingers in the air
Sometimes it bumps me
Sometimes it trips me
Why can't I tell
When it is there.

Stream #17

Perplexing problems posing potential hazards for emerging nations under god-like influences nowhere to be seen but constantly lead through the whining of illiterate individuals under a self-hypnotic trance never satisfied with what they are themselves but saying they are the perfect human in a state of super consciousness mind expanding awe-inspiring and all-encompassing yet if they stray once it is all over in their eyes.

Death and damnation, Hellfire, the devil, and no chance to have good credit again.

What is religion?

Why is it necessary?

It only produces guilt feelings in people who don't need guilt feelings.

The whole religious doctrine no matter what creed it represents, is thorough hypocrisy. Nothing but hypocrisy.

There is no such thing as a "true" believer. If there were, then he would be God or Christ or Buddha or Krishna or etcetera.

For religion to die out would be mankind's greatest blessing, by God...

78.
Sometimes the words make their way past my subconscious.
Sometimes the words struggle to force their symbols out of the pen.
Sometimes the words will not visualize themselves to me.
Sometimes the words just won't come.

79.
A kick in the ass
A blank verse to pass
A parent you like to sass
A termite and his frass
And a fair-haired lass
All add up to life amongst the natives circling like vultures waiting for the primary feeders to finish with the soul of the daytime nighttime the right time to indulge in the not so clear image of near sighted unbelieving discharged servants standing under a light in Times Square or Market Street Van Ness aware interchange can you make change for a hundred people charging Fort Knox gelatin wrung out of electrifying ambiance clear cut the forest past recognition in lew of what's left it still is mighty nice to be an American I swear I can come back again to be an American. Thankyew, thankyew.

80.
The other night sometime late
A vision came to me
In the form of a lazy dream
With the feel of reality
She/He came to me without a sound
And drifted by my bed many times
She/He tried to wake me
By kissing my head
I finally woke up with a start
I thought I was awake
And viewed a lovely lady/man
Who said the time was late
A lovely incubus/succubus she/he said she/he was
Who had viewed me from afar
I coward 'neath my covers then
And said "I know who you are."
Your name is death most likely
And you've come to take my life
Why not come some other time
And instead pick up my wife

She/he looked at me disdainfully
And said she/he wasn't death
Drifting back she hid her face
And quickly turned and left
I thought I drifted back to sleep
Until I heard a sound
My eyes flashed on a naked girl
Prettier than I've found
She drifted low above my bed
And pulled my covers down
She gently touched me everywhere
Than kissed me very soundly
An apparition you must be
But why the gentle touch
I'll not complain if you are kind
I need you very much
I need you too, that's why I'm here
Just lay back and enjoy
I closed my eyes and sighed deeply
For her I became a toy
The feelings came the feelings went
The night seemed very long
And when we both seemed at our peak
I looked and she was gone
Was it real or was it fake?
Have I viewed TV to long?
Is my mind distorting all things real
And changing right to wrong.

Most likely I will never know
If she was all that real
So now I never go to sleep
I just sit around
Staring at the walls in front of me not daring to move for fear
of missing that lovely, nameless apparition that so tenderly touched
me one night.
Maybe…

81.
Lovely thoughts
Lovely visions
Empty pens
Empty decisions
Girls aplenty
Throbbing tension
Pant pant cough wheeze
Time to get my pension
Again fast
Without much persuasion
One foot in the grave
Left foot first.

Stream #18

Yes, how can one go on with the uncontrollable desire to be as one with so many reaching out with greedy hands grasping reality but speaking unreal thoughts never let out except in confidence to the people least of all the confidence should be spoken to and yet never understood for lack of tact lack of reasoning and lack of the ability to see into the eyes of your fellow man who darts in and out of his life like a frightened mouse with no means of escape except through the mouths of babes infiltrating the underground legions where many fold armies have waged wars of injustice against all who need to be tolerated as they are and not as they should be.

82.
Song/Poem
"A Conflict of Interests"

I'm not your god,
I do not plan for you.
I'm not your guiding light,
I only seem that way (it's true).
There may be others here,
Fabricating lives you haven't got.
I wouldn't lie to you,
The pressure's aged me quite a lot.

I'm not Adonis,
I will not pose for you.
I'm not a super man,
And your Lois Lane won't do.

How come you cling to me,
I see you everywhere I walk.
What I say's not wrong,
But I can't say it while you talk.

Your interests aren't mine to plan anymore,
My interests don't excite me anymore.

Don't try to follow,
Don't try to follow.

I'm not Jesus,
Please do not worship me.
My crown of thorns is gone,
And miracles are few and far between.
My time is over now,
I can't answer your questions anymore.
I kid you not,
Your conscience is a bore.

Your interests aren't mine to plan anymore,
My interests don't excite me anymore.

Don't try to follow,
Don't try to follow.

83.
Song/Poem
"She is an Artist"

I met her at a local bistro,
She asked me if I had nowhere to go,
I got invited to go up to her flat,
A Brownstone is where it's at.

She walked me up some six flights of stairs,
The top apartment with all the skylights was hers,
She wanted me to take off all my clothes,
And stand there and pose.

She is an artist,
She is a painter from Soho.
She is an artist,
She likes to live solo.
She is an artist,
A woman in the mood.
She likes to paint her young men nude.

I stood there dressed in goosebumps and hair,
I asked her for a drink, she had Schnapps or cold beer.
I chose the Schnapps to warm me, I was chilled to the bone,
I thought I wanted to go home.

She started by arranging me, it was quite a scene,
Placing me in positions no one else has ever been.
I began to get aroused, I tried to remain calm,
She said "cool it", and kissed me on the palm.

She is an artist,
She is a painter from Soho.
She is an artist,
She likes to live solo.
She is an artist,
A woman in the mood.
She likes to paint her young men nude.

Out came her charcoal, she sketched me in a flash,
The oil paints were next, she didn't waste a single splash.
About two hours later, she said that she was through,
She said "don't' leave, I'm not through yet, with you".

She is an artist,
She is a painter from Soho.
She is an artist,
She likes to live solo.
She is an artist,
A woman in the mood.
She likes to paint her young men nude.

84.
Song/Poem

One step beyond is all it took
It wasn't long, I didn't look at the laughter beside me.
You came and went before my time,
You're heaven sent to be just mine, I saw your finger pointing towards me.
I fell asleep
I was afraid to keep
The shades pulled up
I kept my cup
Filled to the brim
'Till you came in
Made love to me
I couldn't see
Reality.

We didn't talk when you were here,
I couldn't see but felt you near, the fire inside warned me.
I thought of rain when we first met,
Your hand reached out, I was all wet, my passion consumed me.
I fell asleep
I was afraid to keep
The shades pulled up
I kept my cup
Filled to the brim
'Till you came in
Made love to me
I couldn't see
Reality.

The rain outside was flooding town,
Been up so long it looks like down, the muse is watching over me.
I saw a man wet to his skin,
The door was closed, I was not in, I didn't want me to see me.
It's such a tangled web I weave,
Then I felt you slide away to leave, it starts to awaken Me.
I settled back to meditate,
I wondered if I'd ever wake, and if you were really beside me.
I fell asleep
I was afraid to keep
The shades pulled up
I kept my cup
Filled to the brim
'Till you came in
Made love to me
I couldn't see
Reality.

85.
Cornucopia of Earthly Delights

Largely at fault
Remaining intact
Taste of success
Last of the fact
Never asunder
Purpose unknown
Keeping the wonder
Fuses have blown up in the maelstrom envy mass energy warp drive connoisseur driving forces left undone under the faction of reaction purpose of won't cannot will not positive can will not positive will make the summit apex zenith unsurmountable odds making forcing closure of the ending society manages the sway of empires concrete forcing grass break through deteriorate and start again
The end
The beginning
The crux of the matter seeming unperturbed by the thought of anger dangerous points of contact default indebted to the minions millions mutons out of light contact release envy lust might is right is wrongdoing dong long time feel good
Understood

Cornucopia of earthly delights consorting to the overthrow of many delightful table scraps thrown to the dog to the end to the deferment comprehending any tendency to indulge in the wasteful wanton lust of laborious individuals circulating under false names ideas principals' accusations swinging singles

The dream not the reality surfaces under any hot desires looming up in the distance cramming the hot to trot likeness under the covers wont not covet greed need desire free what goes forth to never return is it the sage long sought for never realized who damages souls to repair egos or is it the prophet never certain under age overzealous creating no good by good endeavors searching always groping for the final solution that is death and death alone will surface when destiny deems and seems eminent in life as the producer of energy that will never stop flowing growing

Partly fault of ours never everyone

Those words cannot express the concern, the doubt

Reason to indulge

Creating, promoting

Energy speech line main line

In the end to find out

In the end to work it out

In the end death will erase all doubt in the individual therapy concerning one and many times over the falls sorting it out into intelligent meaning feeling concern again said again felt out in others complaining about their existence and their relationships with those around ego endeavors betray trust bullshit trouble words well-meaning only to one two three and after that what grates you most creating uneasy tension surfaces under the skin as a cancerous tumor timid soul kept at bay by words of prey after the source constantly at the thoughts of each well-meaning busy individual truth seeker dream weaver

Soothsayer, death dealer

Kept on the pedestal of sand washing away slowly under the tide

Soaking shrinking

Dissolve

Disappear

The unsolved mystery of lives ever changing

Ever changing.

86.
Song/Poem

"Ladies"

Ladies, I want to hear you call me,
On the phone sometime, I need to hear a friendly voice.
Ladies, why don't you come on over,
I have wine and many cheeses, come and make your choice.

Ladies, I know you're out there,
I can feel your presence everywhere I go.
Ladies, my body's humming,
From the tunes your gentle voices tend to throw.

You can pick out any song to play on my stereo,
You can see any movie you want on my video,
You can dance, you can sing, you do anything, it's alright with me,
Just stay awhile and do things naturally.

Ladies, I'll never leave you,
Out in the cold somewhere with nowhere else to go,
Ladies, I'm very faithful,
To every one of you, that's something you should know.

I won't ask you to do anything you don't want to do,
I won't touch, I won't curse, I won't dress up like a nurse in front of you,
I just bought Godiva chocolates for your afternoons,
What more could you want, don't go leaving soon.

Come on home tonight,
I'll treat you right,
And meet my mother too.

Ladies, come on home tonight,
I'll treat you right,
And meet my mother too.

87.
The temperamental artist in us craves for release,
The drive to do better is nature's release.
Sometimes the death of a muse finds us depressed and down,
Its rebirth's not much better, it's a thorny crown.

On our heads,
Sometimes dead,
Sometimes alive,
Always striving,
To do well,
What the hell!
What the hell!
What the hell!

A temperamental artist begins work once again,
He has paintings of love and guilt he shows now and then,
He works in mixed media that he's anxious to show,
But he's embarrassed by criticism, that's quite a blow.

To his head,
Sometimes dead,
Sometimes alive,
Always striving,
To do well,
What the hell!
What the hell!

The artistic ego dwells,
Somewhere between,
The man and the scene,
The silence, the scream,
The good and the mean,
The real and the dream.
What the hell, what the hell!

Temperamental artists, with experimental sounds,
If it's not in the top 40, it won't get around,
Commerciality's our enemy, we don't get involved,
But throw us a sheckle or two, our problems could be solved.

Ease our heads,
Sometimes dead,
Sometimes in love,
Always striving,
To do well,
What the hell!
What the hell!

A temperamental artist typing far into the night,
With hopes to be like Kerouac, he tries with all his might,
He started out on coffee, and now he's on the port,
He worries 'bout success too much, he thinks his life's too
short.

It's in his head,
Sometimes dead,
Sometimes in love,
Always striving,
To do well.
What the hell!
What the hell!
What the hell!

The artistic ego dwells,
Somewhere between,
The man and the scene,
The silence, the scream,
The good and the mean,
The real and the dream,
What the hell, what the hell!

Temperamental artists, wherever you are,
Here's to temperamental artists, whoever you are.
Temperamental artists, wherever you are,
Here's to temperamental artists, whoever you are.
Temperamental, temperamental, temperamental,
Temperamental artists.

88.
The hardest to find,
Someone in find,
Hopes for bliss,
Hit or miss.
A hand in the pot,
Calling the shots,
Seen but not heard,
Shouting every word.
A grand old man,
With his pen in hand,
Hopes for bliss,
Hit or miss.
Ancestral traits,
Stay too late.
Seen but not heard,
Shout every word.
No way to ease the noise,
No way to please the boys.
Wrapped up in thought,
Buying or bought,
Hope for bliss,
Hit or miss.
Unnatural acts,
S and M blood pacts.
Seen but not heard,

Shout every word.
Honor of sorts,
Related to sports.
Hopes for bliss,
Hit or miss.
Taken aside,
Something has died.
Seen but not heard,
Shout every word.

89.
Song/Poem

"Life Can Be Hard"

It's the combination of you and I,
That won't unlock the passion, trapped behind our eyes,
It became so obvious, it was just a dream,
We had together, it fit into the scheme
Of things.

Life can be hard, life can be hard,
Go draw your own conclusions,
Life can be hard, life can be hard,
It adds to your confusion,
Life can be hard, life can be hard,
You can't get inspiration,
Life can be hard, life can be hard,
Where's your imagination.

You know all the comfort you gave to me,
Now lies disguised as hospitality.
Our hesitation condemned the love,
It's time to leave now that push has come to shove.

And she said,

Life can be hard, life can be hard,
Go draw your own conclusions,
Life can be hard, life can be hard,
It adds to your confusion,
Life can be hard, life can be hard,
You can't get inspiration,
Life can be hard, life can be hard,
Where's your imagination.

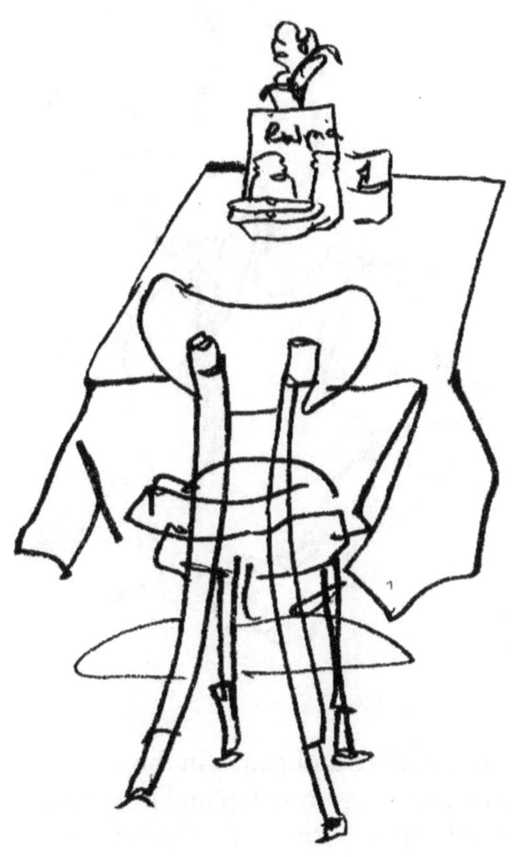

90.
Are you as I see you?
What are you hiding?
The lady I've got to believe in
Is the one that I hardly know.
We seldom talk to each other.

91.
With one to the other and peace in their eyes
And the world at your doorstep and a roomful of flies
Where it works up the thirst of a thousand hot tongues
We had better begin while everyone's young.

92.
I have sought out the few
I have driven them through
The gates where they'll never return
Out from the past
Not one of them last.

93.
Song/Poem
"I Wanna Be a Gigolo"

You're here again,
Holding on to your man,
I've seen you fall from grace,
It's written on your face.

It's so confusing,
You say it's your own choosing,
He's not on your side,
He's taking you for a ride.

'Cause he's a gigolo,
Just a gigolo,
It really shows,
He's a gigolo.

I watch you kiss his lips now,
He drinks you down with sips now,
He wants some money,
To make his nose feel funny (ha, ha, ha).

You buy his clothing,
You even pay for his bowling,
What's he give to you?
Here's a clue:

He's a gigolo,
Just a gigolo,
We all know,
He's a gigolo.

I've watched some time now,
I shake my head and sigh now,
I see myself in his place,
Your lips are kissing my face.

I wanna be a gigolo,
I wanna be a gigolo,
Like your beau,
I wanna be a gigolo.

94.
My glass is empty again.
Have you ever thought of how many glasses you have emptied
in your lifetime so far?

95.
I saw a lady who I wished to meet
She was alone
I dared not present myself to her for fear of rejection
I would be happy just for a smile.

Stream #19

The master has returned his favors for a mover conventional exposure with a little more excess often the real life and death struggle was undermined to revel the intention of one and the invitation of another star-crossed lover left out in the cold.

96.
It will be sometime
Before you reach your prime
And I will be past mine
When we reach that day
What more can I say?

97.

When I reach that age
When a page is just a page
And the light of night reaches
   Out to bury us
Keep your hands at bay
For a chance for me to stay.

98.
Whisper to her again.
Show her quietly what you want and feel from her.
Hide with her again.
The coast is clear to go your way and meet with her.
Greet her.
Speak with her to say what you've wanted to tell someone all
along.
Love her.
Lay with her.
The dream recurs so often there is not a chance it could be
wrong.

99.
Look at me now
Relishing the looks
    And stares
Smiling back
    Like I've never done before.

Stream #20

Many fold inquiries reaching past and beyond reaching the next life exit through the rear-view mirrors reflect what can be or what is not.

Ron Cook is an author, artisan luthier and craftsman living in Santa Cruz, California. He has appeared in, and written for, Renaissance Magazine, and his works have appeared in American Woodworker, American Craft, Early Music America, Dulcimer Players News, Crafts Report, Guitarmaker, Sunset, and several technical trade journals. He and his artistic creations have appeared on television: WABC in New York, KGO in San Francisco, San Jose Community TV, and Community Television of Santa Cruz.

As a craftsman, he uses sustainably harvested, salvaged, and urban forest woods to create one-of-a-kind medieval and Early American stringed instruments, furnishings and sculptures. Distinctive carvings, often known for their subtle humor, are the hallmark of his works and include figures researched from history and legend, as well as from subjects observed in daily life.

Ron exhibited nationally at American Craft Council Shows, and his pieces have been shown in galleries and events as far away as Barcelona, Spain, and are in collections throughout the world.

Ron is a founding member of the Santa Cruz Woodworkers, a 40+ year member of the Guild of American Luthiers, a member of the Santa Cruz Art League, and a Santa Cruz County Open Studios artist for nearly 20 years.